Sojourner Truth: A Voice For Freedom
921 TRU   393

McKissack, Pat

CARLOCK ELEMENTARY

Great African Americans

Sojourner Truth

a voice for freedom

Revised Edition

Patricia and Fredrick McKissack

Series Consultant
Dr. Russell L. Adams, Chairman
Department of Afro-American Studies, Howard University

Enslow Publishers, Inc.

40 Industrial Road	PO Box 38
Box 398	Aldershot
Berkeley Heights, NJ 07922	Hants GU12 6BP
USA	UK

http://www.enslow.com

To Ruth Ella and Charles Wood

Revised edition of *Sojourner Truth: A Voice for Freedom* © 1992

Library of Congress Cataloging-in-Publication Data

McKissack, Pat, 1944–
    Sojourner Truth : a voice for freedom / Patricia and Fredrick McKissack.— Rev. ed.
        p. cm. — (Great African Americans)
    Includes index.
    ISBN-10: 0-7660-1693-5
    1. Truth, Sojourner, d. 1883—Juvenile literature. 2. African American women—Biography—Juvenile
literature. 3. African American abolitionists—Biography—Juvenile literature. 4. Abolitionists—United
States—Biography—Juvenile literature. 5. Social reformers—United States—Biography—Juvenile
literature. [1. Truth, Sojourner, d. 1883. 2. Abolitionists. 3. Reformers. 4. African Americans—Biography.
5. Women—Biography.] I. McKissack, Fredrick. II. Title.
    E185.97.T8 M37   2001
    305.5'67'092—dc21
                                                                                    00-012420

ISBN-13: 978-0-7660-1693-4

Printed in the United States of America

10 9 8 7 6 5 4

To Our Readers
We have done our best to make sure all Internet Addresses in this book were active and appropriate when we went to press. However, the author and the publisher have no control over and assume no liability for the material available on those Internet sites or on other Web sites they may link to. Any comments or suggestions can be sent by e-mail to comments@enslow.com or to the address on the back cover.

Every effort has been made to locate all copyright holders of materials used in this book. If any errors or omissions have occurred, corrections will be made in future editions of this book.

TABLE OF CONTENTS

Sojourner Truth
Born 1797–November 26, 1883

CHAPTER 1

Never Lie. Never Steal. Trust in God.

 ojourner Truth's real name was Isabella. "Slaves didn't have last names," she said. "I was just called Belle."

Belle was born sometime in 1797 in Hurley, New York. Her mother, Mau-Mau Bett, and father, Baumfree, were slaves owned by a Dutch farmer.

Belle was the youngest of nine children. Her brothers and sisters had been sold as slaves to other masters. Belle's mother never knew when

Belle and her brothers and sisters were sold at slave auctions like this one.

Belle would be sold. So she told Belle three rules that would help her when she was on her own: Never lie. Never steal. Trust in God.

When Belle was eleven years old, she was sold away from her parents. Until then, Belle spoke only Dutch. Her new master spoke only English. She could not understand her master's orders. The master's wife beat Belle to make her speak English. The girl tried. But English words were hard to learn. In time Belle learned English, but she always spoke with a Dutch accent.

Belle was sold twice more. In 1810, she was sold to a farmer named John Dumont from New Paltz Landing, New York. She stayed with the Dumonts for seventeen years.

Posters listed the names of slaves for sale.

Belle felt alone during this time. Her mother and father died, and her brothers and sisters had been sold away.

Belle was forced to marry Thomas, an older slave owned by Dumont. In 1815 her first child, Diana, was born. Over the next twelve years she had four other children: Elizabeth, Hannah, Peter, and Sophie.

Belle never knew when one of her children would be sold. So she taught all of them the same things Mau-Mau Bett had taught her: Never lie. Never steal. Trust in God.

CHAPTER 2

"A Slave No More"

ew York State passed a law in 1817 that freed some slaves. The law said that most slaves would be freed on July 4, 1827. Dumont told Belle he would set her free a year early if she agreed to work extra hard. She planted corn, harvested the crops, and hauled buckets of water.

But Dumont didn't free Belle. He did not keep his promise. He said she had not worked hard enough. That's when Belle decided to run away. "I'll be a slave no more," she said. Belle took her baby

**Belle had
hoped
to gain her
freedom
early
by working
hard.**

daughter, Sophie, and ran away. She was helped by a Quaker family. Quakers are a religious people who are against slavery and war.

Dumont followed Belle. He was going to force her to go back. The Quakers offered to pay $20 for Belle and $5 for the baby. Dumont agreed. Belle's new masters freed her and the baby right away.

Belle trusted other slaves to take care of her children when she ran away.

After Belle left, her son Peter was sold. He was just five years old. Peter was now a slave in Alabama. But the law said no slave in New York could

**Belle's young son Peter was sold to a master in Alabama.
The trip south was terrible for slaves, who were forced to walk.**

be sold to someone in a different state. Belle went to a judge to get her son back. The chances of her winning were small, but the judge did give Peter back to his mother. It was a very important case because a black woman had won.

11

CHAPTER 3

From Belle to Sojourner

elle and Peter moved to New York City. She left Sophie with her other daughters, who were still owned by the Dumonts. Belle and the Dumonts had become more friendly. She soon found a job as a housekeeper with the help of other friends. She also gave her time to help the homeless women of New York.

Belle and Peter lived in New York for many years. Peter was in trouble all the time. Then he became a sailor. He wrote to his mother often. But Belle could not read or write.

Friends read Peter's letters to her. The letters stopped coming in 1841. She never heard from him again. Belle began to grow tired of the city. Soon, she decided to leave.

In the 1840s, slaves were treated like animals. They had no rights. Women did not

Even in the 1840s, New York City was a very busy place.

In New York City, Belle joined a number of religious groups.

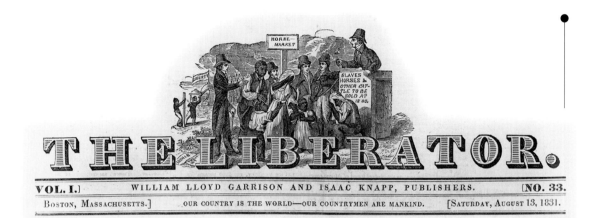

THE LIBERATOR.

VOL. I.]   WILLIAM LLOYD GARRISON AND ISAAC KNAPP, PUBLISHERS.   [NO. 33.

BOSTON, MASSACHUSETTS.]   OUR COUNTRY IS THE WORLD—OUR COUNTRYMEN ARE MANKIND.   [SATURDAY, AUGUST 13, 1831.

have many rights either. They were not allowed to vote. They could not be elected to serve in the government, either.

Many people in New England spoke out against slavery. Some also spoke out for women's rights. Sojourner met these people in her travels. She decided to become a speaker against slavery and for women's rights.

First, she changed her name. She chose *Sojourner* for her first name. A sojourner is a person who travels from place to place. She chose *Truth* as

Articles in The Liberator newspaper were written by people who wanted to put an end to slavery.

a last name because she planned to tell the truth wherever she spoke.

In 1850, Sojourner told her story to Olive Gilbert, who wrote it down. The book was called **Sojourner's book told what it was like to be a slave.** *The Narrative of Sojourner Truth.* When she traveled, Sojourner sold copies of the book to pay her way.

NARRATIVE

OF

SOJOURNER TRUTH;

A Bondswoman of Olden Time,

Emancipated by the New York Legislature in the Early Part of the Present Century;

WITH A HISTORY OF HER

LABORS AND CORRESPONDENCE

DRAWN FROM HER

"BOOK OF LIFE."

BATTLE CREEK, MICH.:
PUBLISHED FOR THE AUTHOR.
1878.

SOJOURNER TRUTH,
"THE LIBYAN SIBYL."

CHAPTER 4

Sojourner Tells the Truth

I n October 1850, Sojourner went to a women's rights meeting in Worcester, Massachusetts. She shocked everyone when she said, "Sisters, I aren't clear what you be after. If women want any rights more than they got, why don't they just take them, and not be talking about it?"

In 1851, Sojourner went to Akron, Ohio,

to speak at another women's rights meeting. Several men spoke before she did. They said women were too weak to be equal to men. But Sojourner knew she had worked as hard as any man. She told them about her years as a slave, working

Elizabeth Cady Stanton, left, was a leader for women's equality.

Sojourner believed that women should stand up for their rights.

18

hard planting and harvesting, and then asked, ". . . aren't I a woman?"

One preacher argued that males were favored by God because Jesus was a man. Sojourner asked: "Where did Jesus come from?" Then she answered her own question out loud. "Jesus came from God and a woman. Man had nothing to do with it!"

Sojourner was very smart. She was also very funny. One man shouted: "What you have to say is no more important than a gnat." "Well," answered Sojourner, "then I hope to keep you scratchin'!"

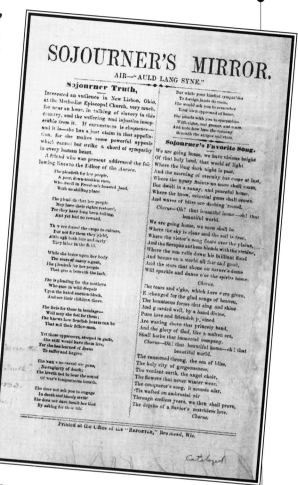

Sojourner liked to include songs and hymns in her speeches.

Many people didn't like what Sojourner was saying. Sometimes her life was in danger.

FREE LECTURE!

SOJOURNER TRUTH,

Who has been a slave in the State of New York, and who has been a Lecturer for the last twenty-three years, whose characteristics have been so vividly portrayed by Mrs. Harriet Beecher Stowe, as the African Sybil, will deliver a lecture upon the present issues of the day,

At   On

And will give her experience as a Slave mother and religious woman. She comes highly recommended as a public speaker, having the approval of many thousands who have heard her earnest appeals, among whom are Wendell Phillips, Wm. Lloyd Garrison, and other distinguished men of the nation.

☞ At the close of her discourse she will offer for sale her photograph and a few of her choice songs.

CHAPTER 5

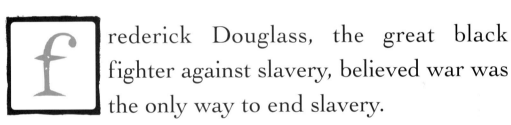

Freedom!

rederick Douglass, the great black fighter against slavery, believed war was the only way to end slavery.

After a meeting where Douglass spoke about ending slavery with a war, Sojourner asked Douglass, "Is God dead?" She was still hopeful slavery would end with the help of God.

The Civil War did start in 1861. The southern states wanted to be separate from the Union. The northern states wanted to keep the country together. Thousands of soldiers fought and died between 1861 and 1865.

In 1863, President Abraham Lincoln freed slaves in the South with the Emancipation Proclamation.

During the Civil War, Sojourner lived in Battle Creek, Michigan. All four of her daughters had married. Two of them, Elizabeth Banks Boyd and Diana Corbin, moved to Battle Creek, too.

Sojourner was older, but she was still very busy. She went to Washington, D.C., with her grandson, Sammy Banks, in June 1864. There she met President Lincoln. They talked for a while.

Frederick Douglass was another former slave who spoke out against slavery.

22

Sojourner was very glad when President Lincoln freed the slaves.

This painting shows Sojourner's visit with President Lincoln in 1864.

Then President Lincoln signed Sojourner's "Book of Life," an autograph book.

He wrote: "For Aunty Sojourner Truth, October 29, 1864." And he signed it "A. Lincoln."

Sojourner stayed in Washington. She was asked to help run the Freedmen's Hospital there. Former slaves, who were called freedmen, came there to be treated for all kinds of illness.

President Lincoln was killed in 1865.

Many men who had been slaves fought in the Civil War on the side of the North.

Sojourner was deeply saddened, but she continued to speak out to help the newly freed slaves.

The Freedmen's Bureau was started to help people who had been slaves. These women learned how to sew.

Sojourner traveled around the country raising money to help them. She had a plan to give unused lands in the West to former slaves. This way they could care for themselves. But the plan never happened.

Sojourner lived the last years of her life in Battle Creek, Michigan. Her daughter Diana Corbin, below, helped care for her.

Sojourner fought for the rights of African Americans until she was too tired and too old to do any more. She went back to Battle Creek, Michigan, in the 1870s. There she lived surrounded by loving family and friends until she died in 1883.

27

In 1986, the U.S. Postal Service issued a stamp to honor Sojourner Truth.

Sojourner Truth

22

Black Heritage USA

timeLine

1797 ～ Born in Hurley, New York.

1814 ～ Marries Thomas, another slave.

1826 ～ Escapes to freedom with her baby daughter.

1828 ～ Moves to New York City.

1843 ～ Changes her name to Sojourner Truth.

1850⊙ ～ Publishes *The Narrative of Sojourner Truth*.

1851 ～ Gives her famous speech at a women's rights meeting.

1864 ～ Meets with President Abraham Lincoln; works for the Freedmen's Bureau in Washington, D.C.

1865 ～ Works in the Freedmen's Hospital.

1883 ～ Dies in Battle Creek, Michigan.

WORDS TO KNOW

civil war—A war fought within a country. The United States Civil War was fought between the northern states and the southern states from 1861 to 1865.

Dutch—The language and people of the Netherlands, a country in Western Europe. The Dutch were the first to settle New York.

Emancipation Proclamation—A ruling written by President Abraham Lincoln that freed all slaves in southern states as of January 1, 1863.

freedmen—The name given to freed slaves.

president—The leader of a country, business, or group.

Quakers—A Christian group known as the Society of Friends. They are a peaceful people who are opposed to slavery and war.

slave—A person who is owned by another and made to work without pay.

sojourner—A person who stays in a place for a short time before moving on again.

Learn more about Sojourner Truth

Books

Adler, David A. *A Picture Book of Sojourner Truth*. New York: Holiday House, Inc., 1996.

Jaffe, Elizabeth Dana. *Sojourner Truth*. Minneapolis, Minn.: Compass Point Books, 2001.

McLoone, Margo. *Sojourner Truth*. Danbury, Conn.: Children's Press, 1997.

Rockwell, Anne F. *Only Passing Through: The Story of Sojourner Truth*. New York: Alfred A. Knopf, 2000.

Internet Addresses

Sojourner Truth
Photos, biography, and more
<http://www.geocities.com/Athens/Oracle/9840/sojourn.html>

National Women's Hall of Fame: Sojourner Truth
Short biography
<http://www.greatwomen.org/women.php?action=viewone&id=158>

Gifts of Speech: Ain't I a Woman?
Sojourner Truth's famous speech
<http://gos.sbc.edu/t/truth.html>

index